Gluten Free
Yeast Free Breads

Kathy Addis

To learn more about baking gluten free, Visit me at: YourGlutenFreeKitchen.com.

Contents

Don't think you have time to make bread?

Yeast type breads are labor intensive and very time consuming. Quick breads, on the other hand, or just what their name implies. Quick and easy and ready in a fraction of the time of yeast breads.

Warm, yummy and delicious, all you need to do is measure, mix and bake!

Imagine starting your day with a basket of hot fresh muffins, or a slice of warm bread; the butter melting as you spread it on. Or cut yourself some slices and spread with softened cream cheese for a wonderful tea time treat.

These are perfect for beginning cooks and the more accomplished baker. With lots of recipes to choose from, there's no reason not to indulge in fresh, hot breads any time of the day.

You'll just love the tantalizing variety of these blue-ribbon recipes. You're sure to find new favorites along with the comfort of old stand byes.

You don't need to stock much in your pantry for these either. Just gluten free flour, salt, liquids like milk or juice, baking powder, baking soda, xanthan gum and eggs. Oil, butter or shortening and honey, maple syrup or sugar.

Then it's up to you to personalize them with fruit, nuts, flavorings, shredded vegetables, herbs and spices.

Don't wait for a special occasion to bake warm-from-the-oven breads.

Indulge yourself and your loved ones today.

Make the perfect loaf of bread

Follow these guidelines:

Grease the bottoms only of loaf pans.

Or use parchment paper slings.

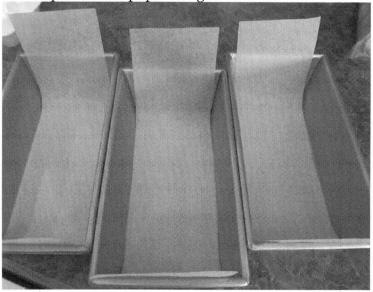

Cut a piece of parchment the width of your loaf pan and long enough so the ends will extend 2" inches on either side when the batter is poured in. Then there is no need to grease the pan at all. You can also allow the loaf to cool completely before you take the bread out as the parchment will just lift it right out. This is my preferred way to bake breads.

Use pans that are longer and narrower than square. An 8x4 loaf pan will bake up better than a 9x5 loaf pan. Using a small 7" Bundt pan for a single loaf of bread will also bake better than a 9x5 loaf pan. Gluten free bread batter is thick and heavier than its non-gluten counterpart. Bundt pans allow hot air to circulate in the middle too, baking the bread better and faster. My preferred loaf pan size is a 10x 4 ¾ pan I found at Home Goods. It bakes a perfect loaf of bread every time.

If the pans you use are dark instead of shiny, reduce the oven temperature down 25 degrees as dark pans absorb the heat and retain it much better than shiny pans do.

Don't be afraid to try baking your batter in Texas sized muffin tins, regular muffin tins or in small loaf pans. All of these will work well with any of the bread recipes here. Just make sure to adjust your baking times accordingly.

Regular loaf pan: 55 to 65 minutes

Small 7" Bundt pan: 43 to 47 minutes

Small loaf pans: 35 to 40 minutes

Texas sized muffin tins: 30 to 35 minutes

Regular muffin tins: 20 to 25 minutes

Mini muffin tins: 15 to 20 minutes

If your bread seems to be browning too fast and looks like it might burn, cover the top with a large piece of aluminum foil, and finish baking.

Always check your breads with a toothpick inserted near the center. If it comes out clean, the bread is done.

Have all ingredients ready to go before hand: this includes chopping or shredding fruit, vegetables or nuts called for in a recipe.

You can either mix by hand or use a hand held electric beater.

Make sure to preheat the oven and prepare all pans or tins before you mix the batter.

Allow the breads to cool before trying to remove from the pan.

Large loaves need 10 minutes.

Small loaves and muffins need 5 minutes

Cool the loaves or muffins completely before packing away to store.

Bread loaves will slice better if allowed to sit overnight, tightly wrapped in the refrigerator.

Use a bread knife to slice your bread loaves. Regulars knives are too harsh and do not have the teeth necessary to cleanly slice through the bread.

All breads will last about 2 days at room temperature, 5 days in the refrigerator, and 4 months in the freezer. Allow to thaw on the counter before serving. You may heat the bread up by placing in a 350 degree oven for 5 to 10 minutes after thawing.

Go ahead and mix your dry ingredients the night before. Then all you have to do is stir in the wet ingredients and pop in the oven for fresh hot bread for breakfast.

Breads

Apple Rhubarb Bread

- ¾ cup chopped rhubarb (fresh or frozen) chopped very small
- ¾ cup chopped peeled apples (about 1) chopped very small
- ¾ cup sugar
  ¼ cup oil, your choice
- 1 tsp. gluten free vanilla
- 2 eggs
- 1 ½ cups gluten free flour blend

- 1 ¾ tsp. baking powder
  1 tsp. salt
- 1 tsp. xanthan gum (omit if flour blend has it already)
- 1 tsp. ground cinnamon

Preheat your oven to 350 degrees.

Make a parchment or foil sling (see directions) and place in the 8x4 loaf pan. Set aside.

Use an electric hand mixer and beat the sugar, oil, vanilla and eggs together. Stir in the rhubarb and apples.

Place all the dry stuff in another bowl and whisk to combine (don't want baking powder blobs in our bread). Stir in to the fruit and pour into your pan.

Bake for 50 minutes or until a toothpick in the center comes out clean.

Let it cool for 10 to 15 minutes. Then pull on the "sling" and pop it out.

Place on a wire rack to cool completely.

Makes 12 slices

Will keep fresh, tightly wrapped, for 4 days out on the counter. You can freeze it forever almost.

For Apple Rhubarb Nut Bread toss in 1/2 cup chopped nuts of choice and stir in with the dry stuff.

Banana Nut Bread

- 5/8 cup sugar
- ¼ cup gluten free organic shortening (Spectrum Naturals…good)
- 1 egg
- ¾ cup mashed bananas (about 2 medium)
- ¼ cup gluten free plain yogurt, sour cream or dairy free buttermilk
- 1 tsp. gluten free vanilla
- 1 ¼ cups gluten free flour blend
- 1 ½ tsp. baking powder
- 1 tsp. xanthan gum (omit if flour blend has it)

- ¼ tsp. salt
- 1/8 tsp. baking soda
- ½ cup chopped nuts, your choice

Preheat your oven to 350 degrees.

Make a parchment or foil sling (see directions) and place in the 8x4 loaf pan. Set aside.

Use an electric hand mixer and beat the sugar and shortening together. Mix in the yogurt, vanilla and egg together. Stir in the bananas (make sure you squished then real good).

Place all the dry stuff in another bowl and whisk to combine (don't want baking powder blobs in our bread). Stir in to the banana batter and then stir in the nuts. Pour into your pan.

Bake for 50 minutes or until a toothpick in the center comes out clean.

Let it cool for 10 to 15 minutes. Then pull on the "sling" and pop it out.

Place on a wire rack to cool completely.

Makes 12 slices

Will keep fresh, tightly wrapped, for 4 days out on the counter. You can freeze it forever almost.

Blue Corn Mini Muffins

- 1 ½ cups stone ground blue cornmeal
- ½ cup gluten free flour
- 1 ½ cups buttermilk
- ¼ cup oil, your choice
- 2 tsp. baking powder
- 1 tsp. sugar
- 1 tsp. salt
- ½ tsp. baking soda
- 2 eggs

Preheat the oven to 450 degrees.

Lightly grease mini muffin tins as set aside.

Whisk together all the dry ingredients together. Mix together the buttermilk, oil and eggs with a fork until blended. Dump the dry ingredients into the buttermilk mix. Stir until no lumps remain.

Fill mini muffin cups about 2/3 full. Bake for 12 minutes or until a toothpick inserted into the center comes out clean. These don't take long.

Let sit for 5 minutes and then pop them out of the tin. You can place them in a lined basket and serve. These are a purple/blue color. Very different. Use these on a buffet table or take with you to a potluck. You could also place these on a plate and cover with chili and cheese.

Makes about 36

Blueberry Oatmeal Bread

This is gorgeous looking bread. I would make this for company because it looks and tastes so good.

- 2/3 cup packed brown sugar
- ¾ cup milk
- ½ cup oil, your choice
- 2 eggs
- 2 ¼ cups gluten free flour
- 1 cup regular or quick certified gluten free oats
- 3 tsp. baking powder
- 1 tsp. ground cinnamon
- ¼ tsp. salt
- 1 cup fresh or frozen blueberries (if you use frozen, thaw and drain well)

Preheat the oven to 350 degrees.

Prepare a parchment "sling" for an 8 ½ x 4 ½ loaf pan.

Beat together the brown sugar, milk, oil and eggs in a large bowl. Add the gluten free oatmeal to the mix and stir in. Let it sit for 5 minutes so the oats have a chance to soak up some of the liquid.

Whisk together the flour, baking powder, cinnamon and salt. Stir into the oat mixture. Fold in the blueberries and pour into the prepared loaf pan.

Bake for 50 to 60 minutes or until a toothpick inserted in the center comes out clean.

Check the bread at about 45 minutes into the baking. If the top looks like it's getting too brown (heading toward burnt!) then cover the top with a piece of foil. Just tear a big one off and lay it gently on top to cover it.

Cool in the pan for 10 minutes. Then just grab the ends of the sling and pull out. Set on a wire rack to cool for another 10 minutes then remove the parchment sling and let it sit to cool completely.

Makes 1 loaf and as many slices as you want (I like mine thick with lots of butter or cream cheese).

Carrot Ginger Bread

- 1 ½ cups finely shredded carrots (about 3)
- ¾ cup sugar
- 1/3 cup oil, your choice
- 2 eggs
- 1 ½ cups gluten free flour
- 1/3 cup finely chopped crystallized ginger
- 2 tsp. baking powder
- 1 tsp. xanthan gum (omit if flour has it)
- ½ tsp. salt
- ½ tsp. ground cinnamon

- ½ tsp. ground cloves

Preheat the oven to 350 degrees.

Prepare a parchment "sling" for an 8 ½ x 4 ½ loaf pan.

In a large bowl, mix together the shredded carrots, sugar, oil and eggs. Whisk the flour, ginger, baking powder, xanthan gum (if using), salt, cinnamon and cloves. Now mix the two together completely.

Pour into the loaf pan and bake for 50 to 60 minutes. Take a toothpick and insert near the center. If it comes out clean, it's done.

Check the bread at about 40 minutes into the baking. If the top looks like it's getting too brown (heading toward burnt!) then cover the top with a piece of foil. Just tear a big one off and lay it gently on top to cover it.

Cool in the pan for 10 minutes. Then just grab the ends of the sling and pull out. Set on a wire rack to cool for another 10 minutes then remove the parchment sling and let it sit to cool completely.

Makes 1 loaf of bread.

This one is really good with cream cheese. Wait till you slice into this and smell that spicy ginger aroma. Heaven.

Cheddar Cheese Bread Sticks

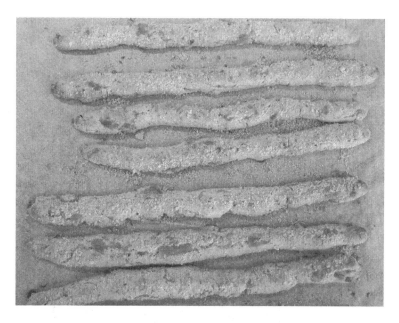

- ¼ cup grated Parmesan cheese
- ½ tsp. paprika
- 2 cups gluten free flour blend
- ½ cup finely shredded Cheddar cheese
- ¾ cup milk
- 2 Tbs. margarine or butter, melted
- 2 tsp. baking powder
- 1 ¼ tsp. xanthan gum
- 1 tsp. sugar
- 1 tsp. salt
- 1 egg, beaten

Mix the Parmesan cheese and paprika together, set aside.

In a large bowl, whisk together the flour, cheddar cheese, baking powder, xanthan gum (if using), sugar and salt. In a small bowl, mix together the milk and the melted butter.

Pour the milk mix into the flour mix and stir together, it will be wet and sticky... good.

Set it aside for 15 minutes. Heat up the oven to 400 degrees.

Place two pieces of parchment paper on the counter. Divide the dough in half, then divide into 12 pieces. Grease up your hands with either olive oil or non-stick cooking spray. Place the first dough ball on the parchment and roll with your hands into a snake the length of the parchment.

Do this for each dough ball until all 12 are rolled out and ready. Take the second piece of parchment and the rest of the dough and do the same.

Using a pastry brush, dip into the beaten egg and brush over the tops of each bread stick. Sprinkle with the Parmesan cheese and paprika.

Pop in the oven and bake for 12 to 15 minutes or until golden brown. Remove from the oven and slide the parchment with the breadsticks off and onto the counter or a wire rack to cool. Serve with more melted butter or marinara sauce.

Munch away.

Chili-Cheese Batter Bread

- 2 cups gluten free flour
- 2 tsp. baking powder
- ¾ tsp. salt
- ¾ tsp. xanthan gum
- ½ tsp. baking soda
- 1 cup shredded Cheddar cheese (about 4 oz.)
- One 4oz. can of diced green chilies
- 1 cup buttermilk
- 1 Tbs. oil, your choice
- 1 egg

Preheat the oven to 350 degrees.

Grease a 9" pie plate and set aside.

Mix together the gluten free flour, baking powder, salt, xanthan gum and baking soda in a large bowl. In a medium bowl whisk together the buttermilk, oil and egg. Stir in the cheese and green chilies. Add all this to the flour mix until no lumps remain and the batter is smooth.

Pour into your pie plate and put in the oven. Bake for 38 to 42 minutes (mine took 40 minutes exactly) or until a toothpick stuck in the center comes out clean.

Take out of the oven and let cool for 10 minutes, pop out of your pie plate and place on a wire rack to cool completely.

Cut into 8 wedges

Chipotle Corn Bread

- 1 ¼ cups stone ground cornmeal (you know, the good stuff)
- ¾ cup gluten free flour
- 1/3 cup oil, your choice
- 1 1/3 cups buttermilk
- 3 Tbs. sugar
- 2 tsp. baking powder
- 1 tsp. salt
- ½ tsp. baking soda
- ½ tsp. ground cumin
- 1 Tbs. finely chopped chipotle chili (Spice Hunter)
- 2 eggs

Preheat the oven to 450 degrees.

Grease either a 9" round pan (can be a pie plate), an 8x8 square pan or a 10" cast iron skillet; set aside.

Mix everything up together in the order listed (I used my electric hand mixer) for about a minute. Pour the batter into your pan of choice.

Bake the 9" round or the square pan for about 25 to 30 minutes. The cast iron skillet only needs about 20 minutes. To make sure it's done, poke a toothpick in the center and make sure it comes out clean.

All done. Now make some chili to go with this and slather on top. Or just spread with soft butter and honey...yum, yum.

If you want, you can add ½ cup of shredded cheese to the batter as well. Or you could toss in ¼ cup cooked, diced bacon. If it was me, I'd probably add both.

Ginger Pear Bread

- 3 cups chopped pears (you can use fresh or a 29oz. can of pears well drained)
- 1 ¼ cups sugar
- ½ cup oil, your choice
- 1 Tbs. finely diced crystallized ginger
- ½ tsp. ground ginger
- 1 egg
- 3 cups gluten free flour
- 3 ½ tsp. baking powder
- 2 ½ tsp. xanthan gum, omit if your flour blend has this)
- 1 tsp. salt

Preheat the oven to 350 degrees. Make a parchment "sling" for two 8x4 loaf pans, set aside.

Mix together the pears, sugar, oil, both gingers and the egg in a large bowl. Whisk together the gluten free flour, baking powder, xanthan gum and salt. Add to the pear mixture and stir well.

Divide between the two loaf pans and pop in the oven. Bake for 45 to 54 minutes (mine took 50 minutes) or until a toothpick inserted in the center comes out clean.

Check your bread loaves at about 35 minutes. If they are getting way too brown on top, cover with a piece of aluminum foil to protect the tops.

Let cool in the pan for about 10 minutes. Then pull up on the parchment sling and place on a wire rack for another 15 minutes. Peel off the parchment and let cool completely.

Makes 2 loaves.

Now, if that seems like way too much ginger for you, just omit the ground ginger. Crystallized ginger is just too good to leave out.

Nutmeg Fig Bread

- 1 ¼ cups gluten free flour
- ½ cup sugar
- ½ cup finely chopped dried figs
- ½ cup buttermilk
- 1/6 cup oil, your choice
- 1 ½ tsp. baking powder
- ¼ tsp. baking soda
- ¼ tsp. salt
- ¼ tsp. ground nutmeg
- 1 egg

Preheat the oven to 350 degrees. Make a parchment "sling" for an 8x4 loaf pan*, set aside.

Toss everything together in a large bowl and beat with an electric hand mixer until combined. Pour into your loaf pan and bake for 38 to 50 minutes (mine took 45 minutes) or until a toothpick inserted in the center comes out clean.

Cool in the pan for 10 minutes and then pull out using the sling. Set on a wire rack and let cool another 15 minutes then pull the parchment off and cool completely.

Makes 1 loaf.

If you want two loaves just double all the ingredients and pour into two loaf pans.

*You can also bake this in a 9" cake pan for 25 to 30 minutes. Unmold onto a cake plate and top with fresh blackberries as seen in the photo.

Chocolate Cherry Loaf

This is a good, moist loaf. I tried baking in a 9x5 loaf pan, but the bread over cooked on the outside and didn't cook all the through the middle. So, I switched it to a 7" bundt pan. It baked up beautifully and in less time than a regular loaf pan.

- 2/3 cup sugar
- ½ cup butter, melted
- ¾ cup milk
- 1 egg
- 1 ½ cups gluten free flour
- ½ tsp. xanthan gum (omit if flour has it)
- 1 cup chopped maraschino cherries, well drained

- ¾ cup gluten free cherry pie filling
- ½ cup semisweet chocolate chips
- 1/3 cup cocoa
- 2 tsp. baking powder
- ¼ tsp. salt

Preheat the oven to 350 degrees. Grease and lightly flour a 7" Bundt pan. Set aside.

Whisk together the sugar, melted butter, milk and egg in a large bowl. Toss in everything and mix well. Pour into the prepared pan.

Bake for 45 to 53 minutes (mine took 48 minutes) or until a toothpick inserted in the center comes out clean. Cool on a wire rack for 10 minutes. Place a cutting board on top of the Bundt pan. Using oven mitts, grab the plate and the Bundt plan and flip it over.

The cake should slide right out. If it doesn't, pick it up and drop down on to the cutting board. It should fall out. Go ahead and let cool completely and then transfer to a serving platter to serve.

Makes 1 Bundt.

You may bake any of the quick bread recipes in a 7" bundt pan. Just follow the times listed above.

Honey Raisin Bread

This one reminds me of "Wheatberry" bread that you can buy in the store. I don't know if they still make it since I can't have any and I haven't looked in a long time, but this reminds me of it. This would make a good toasted sandwich. Pop in your toaster oven and lightly brown the slices. Then top with yummy sandwich fillings.

Takes a little prep work as you need cooked hot cereal.

¾ cup cooked gluten free hot cereal (I used Bob's Red Mill Mighty Tasty Hot Cereal)

- 1 ¼ cups milk

- ½ cup honey or agave or molasses if you want a deeper flavor
- ¼ cup oil of your choice
- 1 tsp. gluten free vanilla extract
- 1 egg
- 3 cups gluten free flour
- 3 tsp. baking powder
- 1 ½ tsp. xanthan gum (omit if flour has it)
- ½ tsp. salt

¾ cup raisins, optional (I did not put in my bread)

Preheat the oven to 350 degrees. Make parchment slings for two 8x5 loaf pans. Set aside

In a large bowl, mix the cooled cooked cereal, milk, honey, oil, vanilla and egg together. In a medium sized bowl whisk together the gluten free flour, baking powder, xanthan gum, salt and raisins.

Add to the milk mixture and stir until combined. Divide the batter into the two loaf pans and bake for 40 to 45 minutes or until done. Cool for 10 minutes on a wire rack. Remove the loaves buy pulling up on the ends of the sling. Place the bread on wire racks to cool completely.

Makes 2 loaves.

You could also bake this in mini loaf pans. This bread freezes well.

Irish Soda Bread

Serve this on St. Patrick's Day for breakfast along with a bowl of steaming gluten free oatmeal topped off with brown sugar and honey.

- 3 tbs. butter, softened
- 2 ½ cups gluten free flour
- 2 Tbs. sugar
- 1 tsp. baking soda
- 1 ½ tsp. baking powder
- 1 tsp. xanthan gum (omit of flour has it)
- ½ tsp. salt

- 1/3 cup raisins (golden are nice but regular ones are more traditional)
- ¾ cup buttermilk

Preheat the oven to 375 degrees. Grease a 9" pie plate and set aside.

Whisk together the flour, sugar, baking soda, baking powder, xanthan gum and salt. Cut in the 3 Tbs. of butter. Or add all the dry ingredients into the work bowl of a food processor. Whiz a few times to combine. Add the butter and whiz a few times until it resembles crumbs or fine sand.

Dump into a bowl and stir in the raisins. Mix in enough buttermilk so it comes together like a biscuit dough. Dump the dough out onto a piece of parchment. Knead with your hands a few times to squish in any stray crumbs. Gently place in the pie plate. Score into 8 pieces with a knife.

Bake for 35 to 45 minutes or until golden brown. Brush the top with softened butter if you want.

Makes 8 slices.

Oatmeal Pineapple Bread

This is really good if you toast the oats first. Spread them in a 9x13 pan and bake at 350 for 15 to 20 minutes. Make sure to stir every 10 minutes.

- ¾ cup sugar
- 1/3 cup organic shortening, melted
- 8 oz. can of crushed pineapple, don't drain – you want the juice
- 2 eggs
- 1 tsp. gluten free vanilla extract
- 1 ¾ cup gluten free flour
- ½ cup golden raisins
- 2 ½ tsp. baking powder

- ½ tsp. xanthan gum
  (omit if flour has it)
- ½ tsp. salt
- ¼ tsp. baking soda
- 1 cup quick cooking gluten free oats
- ½ cup shredded coconut

Preheat the oven to 350 degrees. Prepare a sling for an 8x5 loaf pan, set aside.

In a large bowl, stir together the sugar, shortening, eggs, vanilla and pineapple with juice. In a medium sized bowl, whisk together the flour, baking powder, xanthan gum, salt and baking soda. Stir into the pineapple mixture until combined.

Add the oats and raisins and pour into the loaf pan.

Bake for 55 to 60 minutes or until the loaf tests done. Cool on a wire rack for 10 minutes and then pull the bread out of the pan using the ends of the sling.

Place on a wire rack and cool completely.

Nut Bread

This is just your basic nut bread recipe. Simple and delicious.

- 1 ¼ cups gluten free flour
- ½ cup chopped pecans, or any chopped nut you like
- ¼ cup brown sugar
- ¼ cup granulated sugar
- ½ cup and 2 Tbs. milk
- 3 Tbs. oil, your choice
- 1 ½ tsp. baking powder
- ½ tsp. salt

- ½ tsp. xanthan gum (omit if your flour has it)
- 2 eggs. Beaten

Preheat the oven to 350 degrees. Prepare an 8x5 loaf pan with a sling and set aside.

Whisk together the gluten free flour, brown sugar, granulated sugar, baking powder, salt and xanthan gum together in a large bowl. Add the milk, oil, and eggs and whisk until combined. Stir in the pecans.

Pour into the loaf pan and bake for 55 to 60 minutes or until a toothpick tests clean.

Cool for 10 minutes on a wire rack, then lift the bread out using the sling. Set on a wire rack to cool completely.

Makes 1 loaf

Cut into slices and spread with softened cream cheese for a quick snack.

Variations on Nut Bread

You can take the basic Nut Bread, change out a few ingredients or add some and make a completely different bread.

Date Nut Bread:

Add ½ cup chopped dates and stir in with the nuts.

Orange Nut Bread:

Substitute orange juice for the milk, ¼ cup granulated sugar for the brown sugar and add 2 Tbsp. grated orange peel.

Lemon Nut Bread:

Add 1 Tbsp. grated lemon peel

Spice Nut Bread:

Add ¼ tsp. cloves, ½ tsp. cinnamon and ½ tsp. nutmeg

Pecan Almond Bread:

Use pecans for the chopped nuts and add ½ tsp. almond extract.

Pumpkin Bread

A must have during the holidays. If you want to make it any other time during the year, make sure to buy enough canned pumpkin while it's available. I tried to go buy some last year during the summer and couldn't find it anywhere.

- 1 cup sugar
- 1 cup canned pumpkin (not pie filling)
- 1/3 cup oil, your choice
- 1 tsp. gluten free vanilla extract
- 2 eggs
- 1 ½ cups gluten free flour

- ½ cup chopped nuts, optional
- 2 tsp. baking powder
- ½ tsp. xanthan gum
- ½ tsp. cinnamon
- ¼ tsp. salt
- ¼ tsp. ground cloves

Preheat the oven to 350 degrees. Prepare an 8x5 loaf pan with a sling and set aside.

Whisk together the sugar, pumpkin, oil, vanilla and eggs in a large bowl. You can use a hand held electric mixer if you want. Whisk together the gluten free flour, baking powder, xanthan gum, cinnamon, salt and cloves together in a medium bowl.

Toss the flour mixture into the pumpkin and whisk until combined. Pour into the loaf pan and bake for 50 to 60 minutes or until a toothpick testes clean.

Cool for 10 minutes on a wire rack, then lift the bread out using the sling. Set on a wire rack to cool completely

Makes 1 loaf

Pizza Loaf

This is a wonderful bread to serve with a bowl of spaghetti. Or toast lightly, cover with pizza toppings and then toast again and have for lunch or a light dinner. You could also cut this into "sticks" and toast with garlic spread.

- 1 cup milk
- ¼ cup olive oil
- ½ tsp. dried basil
- ¼ tsp. crushed red pepper
- 1 egg
- 2 ¼ cups gluten free flour
- ¾ cup shredded mozzarella cheese
- 1/3 cup chopped pepperoni
- ¼ cup sliced black olives

- 2 Tbs. grated Parmesan cheese
- 3 tsp. baking powder
- 1 tsp. xanthan gum

Preheat the oven to 350 degrees. Prepare an 8x5 loaf pan with a sling and set aside.

In a medium bowl, whisk together the gluten free flour, baking powder and xanthan gum, set aside. Whisk together the milk, oil, basil, red pepper and egg in a large bowl until combined. Add the flour mix and then the mozzarella, olives and parmesan.

Pour into the prepared loaf pan, sprinkle with a little more parmesan cheese, if desired. Bake for 45 to 50 minutes or until a toothpick comes out clean.

Cool for 10 minutes on a wire rack, then lift the bread out using the sling. Set on a wire rack to cool completely

Makes 1 loaf.

Zucchini Bread

Well, you've got to use up all that zucchini somewhere, right?

3 cups shredded zucchini, blotted dry (about 3 medium)

- 1 2/3 cups sugar
- 2/3 cup oil, your choice
- 2 tsp. gluten free vanilla extract
- 4 eggs
- 3 cups gluten free flour
- ½ cup chopped pecans, optional

- ½ cup dried cranberries or golden raisins
- 4 tsp. baking powder
- 1 tsp. xanthan gum
- 1 tsp. salt
- 1 tsp. cinnamon
- ½ tsp. ground cloves

Preheat the oven to 350 degrees. Prepare two 8 ½ x4 ½ loaf pans with a sling and set aside.

Whisk the gluten free flour, baking powder, xanthan gum, salt, cinnamon and cloves together in a medium bowl. Whisk in the pecans and the cranberries, set aside.

In a large bowl, whisk together the sugar, oil, vanilla extract and eggs. Then add the zucchini and then the flour mixture. Pour into the prepared pans.

Bake for 50 to 60 minutes or until a toothpick comes out clean.

Cool for 10 minutes on a wire rack, then lift the bread out using the sling. Set on a wire rack to cool completely

Makes 2 loaves.

This would be a good candidate for using a 10" bundt pan instead of the 2 loaf pans.

Lemon Poppy Seed Bread

- ¾ cup sugar
- 1/3 cup oil, your choice
- 1/3 cup milk
- 2 eggs
- 2 tsp. lemon emulsion flavoring
- 1 ½ cups gluten free flour
- 2 tsp. finely shredded lemon peel
- 2 tsp. baking powder
- 1 tsp. xanthan gum (omit if GF flour has it)
- ½ tsp. salt
- 1 Tbsp. poppy seeds

Preheat the oven to 350 degrees.

Prepare a parchment "sling" for an 8 ½ x 4 ½ loaf pan.

In a large bowl, mix together the sugar, oil, milk and eggs and lemon flavoring. Whisk the flour, lemon peel, baking powder, xanthan gum (if using), salt, and poppy seeds. Now mix the two together completely.

Pour into the loaf pan and bake for 50 to 60 minutes. Take a toothpick and insert near the center. If it comes out clean, it's done.

Gluten Free Cherry Bread Loaf

- ½ cup shortening
- ¾ cup sugar
- 2 eggs
- 1 tsp. gluten free vanilla
- 2 cups gluten free flour
- 1 ½ tsp. xanthan gum (omit if gf flour blend has it included)
- 1 tsp. baking soda
- 1 tsp. baking powder
- ½ tsp. salt
- 1 cup buttermilk
- 1 jar (10oz.) of maraschino cherries, drained and chopped (1 cup)

Preheat the oven to 350 degrees. Line an 8x4 or a 9x5 loaf pan with parchment paper strip. No need to grease.

In a large bowl, add the shortening and sugar and cream with an electric mixer until light and fluffy. Add the eggs and vanilla and beat in well.

Place the gluten free flour, xanthan gum (if using), baking soda, baking powder and salt in a large bowl. Whisk together.

Add ½ the flour mix to the eggs and mix well. Add ½ the buttermilk and mix well. Finish off with the rest of the flour mix and then the buttermilk. Fold in the chopped cherries.

Pour into your loaf pan and bake for 45 to 55 minutes. If your bread is getting too brown on the top, place a piece of aluminum foil over the loaf pan during the last 15 minutes. Test with a toothpick to make sure it is completely cooked in the center.

Allow bread to cool in the pan for 10 minutes. Remove the bread by pulling up on the ends of the parchment paper and then place on a wire rack to cool. Remove the paper after 20 minutes and cool completely.

Store tightly wrapped in the refrigerator. Will keep for 3 to 4 days. Makes 1 loaf.

Cherry Glaze:

Mix 2 Tbsp. of the reserved cherry juice to 1 cup of powdered sugar, stirring together. If it is too stiff, add a little more juice, if too runny add a little more sugar. You can also add 1 tsp. of vanilla as well. Spread on the loaf.

Apple Streusel Bread

- 1 cup finely shredded apples (peel and core first, then shred)
- ¾ cup sugar
- 1/3 cup oil, your choice
- 1/3 cup apple juice or apple cider
- 2 eggs
- 1 ½ cups gluten free flour
- 2 ½ tsp. baking powder
- 1 tsp. xanthan gum (omit if flour has it)
- ½ tsp. salt
- ½ tsp. ground cinnamon
- ½ tsp. ground cloves

Preheat the oven to 350 degrees.

Prepare a parchment "sling" for an 8 ½ x 4 ½ loaf pan.

In a large bowl, mix together the shredded apples, sugar, oil, apple juice and eggs. Whisk the flour, baking powder, xanthan gum (if using), salt, cinnamon and cloves. Now mix the two together completely.

Pour into the loaf pan. Top with the streusel. Bake for 50 to 60 minutes. Cover the top with a piece of foil if it looks like the streusel topping is browning too quickly.

 Take a toothpick and insert near the center. If it comes out clean, it's done.

For the Streusel:

- 3 Tbsp. gluten free flour
- ¼ cup packed brown sugar
- ½ tsp. cinnamon
- ¼ tsp. nutmeg
- ¼ cup chopped nuts, optional
- 2 Tbsp. butter

Mix everything together in a medium sized bowl except the butter. Cut in the butter using a pastry cutter or two knives until mixture is crumbly and the size of green peas. Sprinkle over the loaf before baking.

Dill Caraway Cheese Bread

A great quick bread to use for ham or pastrami sandwiches. You may omit the cheese if you like.

- 1 ½ cups gluten free flour
- 2 tsp. baking powder
- 1 tsp. xanthan gum (omit if flour has it)
- ½ tsp. salt
- 1 tsp. dried dill weed
- 1 Tbsp. caraway seeds
- 1 cup shredded Swiss cheese
- 2/3 cup milk
- 2 eggs
- ¼ cup oil
- 2 Tbsp. honey

Preheat the oven to 350 degrees.

Prepare a parchment "sling" for an 8 ½ x 4 ½ loaf pan.

In a large bowl, whisk together the flour, baking powder, xanthan gum (if using), salt, dill, caraway seeds and shredded cheese. In another bowl, beat together the milk, eggs, oil and honey.

Now mix the two together completely.

Pour into the loaf pan and bake for 50 to 60 minutes. Take a toothpick and insert near the center. If it comes out clean, it's done.

Chocolate Quick Bread

Lightly toast slices of this bread. Top with a scoop of ice cream, pour over hot fudge sauce and top with whipped cream and a cherry.

Or, cut slices into cubes and layer with cherry yogurt. Drizzle with cherry sauce. Or substitute strawberries for the cherries.

- 6 Tbsp. butter
- ½ cup chopped bittersweet chocolate
- ¾ cup sugar
- 1 cup milk
- 1/3 cup oil, your choice

- 1 tsp. vanilla extract
- 2 eggs
- 1 ½ cups gluten free flour
- ½ cup cocoa powder
- 1 tsp. baking powder
- ½ tsp. baking soda
- 1 tsp. xanthan gum (omit if flour has it)
- ½ tsp. salt

Preheat the oven to 350 degrees.

Prepare a parchment "sling" for an 8 ½ x 4 ½ loaf pan.

Melt the butter with the bittersweet chocolate. Stir until smooth. Set aside.

In a large bowl, mix together the sugar, milk, oil, vanilla extract and eggs. Whisk the flour, cocoa powder, baking powder, baking soda, xanthan gum (if using), and salt. Now mix the two together completely. Stir in the melted chocolate mixture.

Pour into the loaf pan and bake for 50 to 60 minutes. Take a toothpick and insert near the center. If it comes out clean, it's done.

Chocolate Frosted Pumpkin Bread

- 1 2/3 cup gluten free flour blend (xanthan gum added)
- 1 tsp. baking soda
- ¾ tsp. salt
- 1 tsp. cinnamon
- ½ tsp. nutmeg
- ¾ cup sugar
- ¾ cup brown sugar, packed
- ½ cup oil
- 2 eggs
- 1/3 cup water
- 1 cup pumpkin puree, not pumpkin pie mix
- 1 ½ Tbsp. butter, softened

- 1 cup powdered sugar
- 2 Tbsp. unsweetened cocoa powder
- ½ Tbsp. milk
- ¼ tsp. cinnamon
- ¼ tsp. instant espresso coffee powder
- ½ tsp. gluten free vanilla extract
- Additional milk

Preheat the oven to 350 degrees. Line a 9x5 loaf pan with parchment paper, making sure the ends hang over so you can lift the bread out. Grease the sides of the pan. Set aside.

Whisk together the gluten free flour blend, baking soda, salt, cinnamon and nutmeg in a medium bowl.

In a large bowl, beat the oil and both sugars together until combined, about 2 to 3 minutes. Beat in both eggs. Add ½ of the flour mixture, beat well. Add ½ the water, beat well. Repeat one more time.

Muffins

Simple steps to great muffins

Make sure to keep the dry and wet ingredients separated until you are ready to bake. That means that the oven must be at the correct temperature and your muffin tins must be ready with either papers or sprayed with non-stick cooking spray.

Always whisk the dry ingredients together to evenly distribute the baking powder and/or baking soda and salt. You don't want small lumps of baking powder or soda in your muffin.

Always beat together the wet ingredients to make sure they are completely mixed before you combine it with the dry ingredients.

If you are using honey or maple syrup (or any liquid sweetener) make sure to slowly beat it in with the other wet ingredients. This will make it a lot easier to beat in.

Allowing the batter to "rest" for 2 minutes will give the leavening agents a chance to get started before you place the muffins in the oven.

Fill any container you are using 2/3rds full to give the batter enough space to rise but not enough to overflow the top edges.

You can use any type of pan you want: mini muffin tins, regular muffin tins, Texas sized muffin tins, square tins or mini loaf pans. All of these will make great muffins; just remember to adjust the baking time depending on the size of the muffin. Mini muffins will bake a lot faster that Texas sized muffins.

Make sure your oven is preheated and ready. You may want to check the temperature on your oven for accuracy. Oven gauges are available to see if your oven heats up to the correct temperature. It is not uncommon for an oven to be off 5 to 10 degrees either way from the dial. This will affect your baking times, so it's a good idea to check your oven and calibrate it if it is off.

When your muffins are done, allow them to cool for 5 minutes and then place on wire racks to cool completely. If you want to keep them warm, you can leave them in the tin. Just pop them out and place sideways in the tin so the bottom doesn't become soggy.

Raisin Bran Muffins

- 1 1/2 cups of certified gluten free oat or rice bran
- 1/2 cup dark raisins
- 1 1/2 Tbsp. baking powder
- 3/4 cup gluten free flour blend
- 1/2 tsp. xanthan gum
- 3/4 tsp. ground ginger
- 3/4 tsp. ground cinnamon
- 3/4 cup dark molasses
- 2 Tbsp. honey
- 1/2 cup hot tap water
- 1 egg
- 1 egg white

Preheat oven to 425 degrees.

Place all the dry ingredients in a large bowl and whisk to combine. In a small bowl, stir together the molasses, honey, water and eggs. Pour into the flour mixture and stir together with a spoon.

Scoop into muffin tins sprayed with non-stick cooking spray until almost full (these do not rise much). Bake for 10-12 minutes or until a toothpick comes out clean. Take the muffins out and cool on a wire rack. Will stay fresh for 4 days in an airtight container.   Makes 12

If you can't eat all the muffins within 4 days, go ahead and freeze the rest.

Wrap each in plastic wrap and place in a freezer bag.

Will stay fresh for 2 months.

Garlic Herb Muffin

Here is a savory muffin that would go well with many things. Soup, gluten free spaghetti and meatballs, chicken, turkey, ham or made into cute little tea sandwiches.

- 1 6.5oz package of Garlic & Herb spreadable cheese, softened (like Alouette)
- 1 egg
- 1 cup milk
- 1/4 cup olive oil
- 2 cups gluten free flour***
- 2 1/2 tsp. baking powder

- 1 tsp. xanthan gum
- 1/4 tsp. salt

*** I used Pamela's gluten free flour blend. This already had xanthan gum, salt and baking powder in it. To use this, don't add xanthan gum, or salt and reduce the amount of baking powder to 1 1/2 tsp.

Preheat the oven to 400 degrees.

Grease muffins wells. I used an 8 well rectangle muffin tin. Makes cute little loaves. Or line them with papers.

Beat the cheese and the egg together with an electric mixer until creamed well. Add the milk and oil and mix together.

Place the gluten free flour, baking powder, and xanthan gum and salt if using and whisk together. Pour into the cheese mixture and either beat with the mixer or stir together by hand. I want it done NOW, so I used the electric mixer.

Scoop out the dough using a cookie scoop and divide among the muffin well

Bake for 20 to 25 minutes (mine took 23). Poke with a toothpick and make sure it comes out clean then pull them out. Pop them out right away or stand them up on their edges to cool. If you leave them in the muffin tin to cool they will get soggy bottoms. Nobody wants soggy bottoms, not even muffins.

Makes 8 rectangles or 12 regular muffins

Banana Oat Muffins

- 1 package gluten free yellow cake mix
- 1 cup certified gluten free quick cooking oats
- 2 ripe bananas
- 1/4tsp. salt
- 3/4 cup milk (or milk alternative)**
- 2 large eggs
- 2 Tbsp. oil, your choice
- Crumble Topping (see below)

Preheat the oven to 400 degrees.

Line 16 muffin tins with papers or grease the muffin cups well. I like to use papers because I think it's easier to clean up, but that's just me.

Make the crumble topping and set aside. Put in the fridge if your kitchen is hot.

Whisk the gluten free cake mix, oats and salt in a large bowl. In a medium bowl, beat together the eggs, milk, bananas and oil using an electric hand mixer for 2 minutes. Add to the dry ingredients and stir just until combined. Fill each muffin cup 2/3rds full (I cheat and use a large cookie scoop).

Now take some of the crumble topping that you made and sprinkle on top of the muffin batter.

Bake for 13 minutes or until a toothpick inserted in the middle comes out clean.

Take out of the oven. If you used papers, let those cool 2 minutes and then pop them out of the tin and set on a wire rack. If you greased and did not use papers, let them cool 4 minutes, run a thin spatula around the sides and slowly pop up and out. Place on a wire rack to cool.

Crumble Topping

You can make a full batch of topping or cut the ingredients in half. If you don't use all the topping, just pop it in a zip top freezer bag and freeze. It will last for a year in the freezer.

- 1 package of gluten free yellow cake mix
- 1 tsp. ground cinnamon
- 1 ½ sticks of butter

Dump the cake mix and cinnamon into the bowl of a food processor. Cut the butter into small cubes and toss in.

Whiz with the pulse button until it resembles coarse crumbs.

**Replace up to 1/4 cup of the milk with applesauce or pear sauce for an added fruity treat.

Almond Muffins

- 1 1/3 cups gluten free flour blend (xanthan gum added)
- ½ cup brown sugar, firmly packed
- 1 tsp. baking powder
- ½ tsp. baking soda
- ¼ tsp. salt
- 1 cup and 2 Tbsp. sliced almonds
- ½ cup buttermilk
- ¼ cup oil
- 2 eggs
- ½ tsp. gluten free vanilla extract
- ½ tsp. gluten free almond extract
- Cinnamon-Sugar for topping

Preheat the oven to 350 degrees. Line muffin tins with paper muffin cups. Set aside

Whisk the gluten free flour, brown sugar, baking powder, baking soda and salt in a large bowl.

Beat together the buttermilk, oil, eggs, and extracts together in a medium sized bowl.

Stir in 1 cup of the almonds into the flour mixture. Pour the liquid ingredients over the flour mixture and stir until completely combined.

Using a large cookie scoop, place dough into the muffin cups.

Sprinkle the tops of the muffins with the remaining 2 Tbsp. of sliced almonds and cinnamon sugar.

Bake for 20 to 25 minutes or until a toothpick inserted in the center comes out clean.

Immediately take out of the muffin tins and place on wire racks to cool completely.

Makes 12 muffins

Double Oat Muffins

- ¾ cup gluten free instant oats
- ¼ cup gluten free oat bran
- ¾ cups gluten free flour blend (xanthan gum added)
- ½ cup sugar
- 2 tsp. baking powder
- ½ tsp. baking soda
- ½ tsp. salt
- ½ cup buttermilk
- 1/3 cup oil
- 2 eggs
- 2 Tbsp. instant oats
- Cinnamon-Sugar for topping

Preheat the oven to 400 degrees. Line muffin tins with tulip papers and set aside.

Whisk together all the dry ingredients except the extra 2 tbsp. of instant oats and the cinnamon-sugar.

Beat together the buttermilk, oil and eggs until well combined.

Add to the flour mixture and stir well.

Using a large cookie scoop, place muffin dough into the papers. Sprinkle with extra instant oats and the cinnamon-sugar.

Place in the oven and bake for 15 to 18 minutes or until a toothpick inserted in the center comes out clean.

Immediately remove the muffins and place on wire racks to cool completely.

Serve with honey butter.

Makes 12 muffins.

Texas Bacon Corn Muffins

- 1 cups gluten free flour blend (xanthan gum added)
- ¾ cup stone ground gluten free cornmeal
- 1 ½ tsp. baking powder
- 1 tsp. sugar
- 1 tsp. salt
- ½ tsp. baking soda
- 1 cup buttermilk
- 1 cup shredded sharp cheddar cheese
- 8 ½ oz. can of gluten free cream style corn
- ¼ cup oil

- 2 eggs, beaten
- 2 Tbsp. diced jalapeno peppers*
- 6 slices of bacon, cooked and crumbled

Preheat the oven to 375 degrees. Spray a 12 cup square muffin tin with non-stick cooking spray. Set aside.

Combine the flour, cornmeal, baking powder, sugar, salt, and baking soda in a large bowl.

Whisk together the buttermilk, cheese, cream corn, oil, eggs, peppers and bacon.

Stir the liquid ingredients into the flour/corn mix until well combined.

Use a medium cookie scoop and place cornmeal dough into the prepared muffin tin.

Bake for 25 to 30 minutes or until a tooth pick inserted in the center comes out clean.

Immediately remove from the muffins from the pan and place on wire racks to cool completely.

Makes 15 muffins.

Since the pan only holds twelve, place 3 foil muffin cups on a small baking sheet and place on the rack below. Bake with the rest.

We reserved 15 of the larger bacon crumbles to place on top of the batter before baking. See the photo.

Sweet Potato Corn Bread

- 1 15 oz. can of sweet potatoes, drained and mashed
- ½ cup buttermilk
- 1/3 cup oil
- 2 eggs
- 1 cup stone ground gluten free cornmeal
- 1 cups gluten free flour blend (xanthan gum added)
- 1/3 cup sugar
- 2 ½ tsp. baking powder
- ½ tsp. baking soda
- 1 tsp. ground cinnamon
- ½ tsp. ground allspice

- ½ tsp. salt

Preheat the oven to 400 degrees. Spray a mini-loaf tin with non-stick cooking spray and set aside.

Beat together in a large bowl, the sweet potatoes, buttermilk, oil and eggs.

Whisk all the dry ingredients together in a medium sized bowl. Stir the flour mixture into the sweet potato mixture until combined.

Using a medium sized cookie scoop, drop two mounds of dough into each mini-loaf section.

Bake for 20 to 24 minutes or until a toothpick inserted in the center comes out clean.

Immediately remove from the mini loaf tin and place on wire racks to cool completely.

Makes 8 mini corn loaves.

Corny Corn Muffins

- 1 cup stone ground gluten free corn meal
- 1 cups gluten free flour blend (xanthan gum added)
- 2 Tbsp. sugar
- 1 Tbsp. baking powder
- ¾ tsp. salt
- ½ tsp. baking soda
- 2 eggs
- ¼ cup oil
- 1 cup shredded cheddar cheese
- 1 cup whole corn, drained
- ½ cup sour cream
- ½ cup buttermilk

Preheat the oven to 375 degrees. Thoroughly grease a mini scone pan. Set aside.

Whisk the corn meal, gluten free flour, sugar, baking powder, salt and baking soda together in a large bowl.

In a medium sized bowl, beat the eggs, oil, cheese, sour cream and buttermilk. Stir in the corn. Stir into the flour mixture until combine d.

Using a small cookie scoop, carefully place the dough into the mini scone pan, using your fingers to gently push into the space.

Bake for 17 to 19 minutes or until a toothpick inserted in the center comes out clean.

Immediately remove the corn bread from the pan, using a mini silicone spatula to aid in removing the corn breads if needed. Place on wire racks to cool completely.

Makes 16 mini corn bread scones

Apple Cream Cheese Muffins

Serve these jumbo muffins hot with honey butter.

- 3 cups gluten free flour blend (one with xanthan gum added)
- 1 Tbsp. baking powder
- 2 tsp. ground cinnamon
- 1 tsp. salt
- 8 oz. cream cheese, softened, divided
- 2 cups sugar, divided
- ¼ tsp. almond extract
- ½ cup canola oil
- 1/3 cup milk
- 2 eggs

- 1 cup peeled and shredded apples (2 medium) Pink Lady's or Honeycrisp or good choices
- Cinnamon sugar

Preheat the oven to 350 degrees. Line 12 jumbo muffin cups with paper liners.

Beat together 4 oz. of the cream cheese, ½ cup of the sugar and the almond extract together in a small bowl. Set aside.

Whisk together the gluten free flour, baking powder, cinnamon and salt in a medium sized bowl. In a large bowl, beat together the remaining 4oz. of cream cheese and the 1 ½ cups of sugar until fluffy. Beat in the oil and milk, and then beat in the eggs. Stir in the shredded apples, and then gradually stir in the flour mixture until everything is combined.

Using a large cookie scoop, portion out the muffin batter into the 12 paper liners. Drop the cream cheese mixture into the center of each muffin. Sprinkle the top with cinnamon sugar.

Bake for 30 to 35mintues or until a toothpick inserted near the center comes out clean.

Makes 12 Jumbo muffins

Pumpkin Streusel Mini Breads

- 1 cup butter, softened
- 1 cup sugar
- 1 cup brown sugar, packed
- 1 tsp. gluten free vanilla extract
- 4 eggs
- 1 15oz. can pure pumpkin puree (not pumpkin pie mix)
- 2 cups gluten free flour blend (one with xanthan gum added)
- 1 ½ tsp. baking powder
- 1 ½ tsp. baking soda
- 1 tsp. ground cinnamon
- ¾ cup buttermilk

Streusel Topping

- ¼ cup certified gluten free quick oats
- 2/3 cup gluten free flour blend (one with xanthan gum added)
- ¼ cup brown sugar, packed
- 1 tsp. ground cinnamon
- ¼ cup butter, cut into cubes

Preheat the oven to 350 degrees. Line 5 mini loaf pans (5x3") with strips of parchment paper. Or spray the loaf pans with non-stick cooking spray. Set aside.

Make the Streusel Topping by combining the oats, 2/3 cup flour, brown sugar and cinnamon in a small bowl. Stir well. Add the butter cubes and use a pastry blender to work in the butter until the mixture is crumbly. Place in the refrigerator while you make the loaves.

In a large bowl, cream together the butter, sugar and brown sugar until light and fluffy. Beat in the eggs, one at a time. Stir in the pumpkin.

In a medium sized bowl, whisk together the gluten free flour blend, baking powder, baking soda and cinnamon.

Beat in a 1/3 of the flour mix into the butter. Then beat in half of the buttermilk. Beat in another 1/3 of the flour followed by the rest of the buttermilk. Beat in the last bit of flour.

Divide the batter among the 5 loaf pans. Sprinkle with the Streusel Topping.

It is usually easier to place the mini loaf pans on a baking sheet and slid this in the oven than trying to get the small loaf pans to sit well on the oven racks.

Bake for 30 minutes or until a toothpick inserted into the center comes out clean. Cool in the pans for 10 to 15 minutes. Run a spatula around the edges of the bread to help loosen. Set on wire racks to cool completely.

Makes 5 mini loaves

Send us your favorite recipes!

Include why this recipe is your favorite and why it is special to you.

If your recipe is selected for one of our upcoming books, we will include your name and home town right in the credits! You will also receive a FREE copy of the book as our thank you!

Mail in your recipes to:

Your Gluten Free Kitchen
c/o cookbook recipes
3808 E 38th Street
Tucson, Az 85713

Make sure to include the number of servings and all other information for the recipe.

Or e-mail them kathy@yourglutenfreekitchen.com
Subject line: cookbook recipes

Sign up for our e-mail list! We have great gluten free giveaways and kitchen gadget giveaways each month, so be sure to join the fun!

How Did Your Gluten Free Kitchen get started?

Your Gluten Free Kitchen was started in 2008 in a small home kitchen in Tucson, Arizona. Having been diagnosed with celiac in 2001, I went in search of good tasting gluten free foods that I could prepare and enjoy. Being disappointed with what was available; I rolled up my sleeves, tied on my apron and got busy in the kitchen coming up with recipes that tasted just as good as the ones I remember.

Growing up with a farm mom, who is a great cook, I received amazing cooking lessons from her which helped me as I began to bring great tasting dishes and desserts to my own gluten free table.

The goal of Your Gluten Free Kitchen is to help you enjoy the bounty of foods available. Let's live life full of the good things that come from our kitchens.

Just like my mother helped me, let me come along side of you and show you how tasty and satisfying gluten free cooking and baking can be.

Kathy

"He makes grass grow for the cattle, and plants for man to cultivate – bringing forth food from the earth… and bread that sustains his heart."

Psalm 104:14, 15

Made in the USA
Columbia, SC
31 March 2023

14583873R00052